MW00951917

RUTH

An Invitation to Hope, in a Land Unknown

Hope Radebaugh

Prayerful Reflections & Illustrations by Dee Kijanko

A NATIONS OF COACHES DEVOTIONAL

RUTH

An Invitation to Hope, in a Land Unknown

Copyright © 2023 Nations of Coaches

ISBN: 9798858880523
Independently published.

All rights reserved.

No part of this book may be reproduced or transmitted in any form or by any means, electronic or mechanical, including photocopying, recording, or any information storage and retrieval system, without permission in writing from the publisher.

Unless otherwise noted, all scriptures are from THE HOLY BIBLE, NEW INTERNATIONAL VERSION®. Copyright© 1973, 1978, 1984 by Biblica, Inc.™. Used by permission of Zondervan.

Front cover image and devotional layout design by Rachel Aponte.
Edited and reviewed by Tanya Cramer.

Contents

Lineage of Jesus

1
Introduction to the Book of Ruth

In the middle of some of the darkest times in the history of the Nation of Israel, a SONbeam bursts forth on the pages of Scripture in the short book of Ruth. This beautiful story, the 8th book of the Old Testament, only four chapters in length, was written during a time in Israel's history when the nation was far away from God, indulged in idol worship, and under the rule and reign of judges.

God had delivered Israel out of 400 years of Egyptian bondage and had brought them into Canaan, the Land of Promise. However, this generation had forgotten God and all He had done for them—ignoring His ways, entrusting their hearts to be managed and cared for by lifeless, helpless idols.

Three hundred years into a climate of spiritual darkness and defeat, a miracle is in the making. Just as "the barley harvest is beginning," (Ruth 1) God, the faithful Promise Keeper, is setting the stage for the earthly bloodline of His Son, Jesus: Israel's promised Redeemer; every believer's promised Redeemer, though He's been forgotten and ignored.

Fulfilling the genealogy of Christ to come, in perhaps the sweetest redemption story ever told, the book of Ruth offers HOPE for what God can and will do in the middle of a "nation's impossible."

The book of Ruth offers HOPE for what God can and will do in the middle of "your impossible."

May you glean from Scripture all that God has for YOU. May you follow Ruth's footsteps—gleaning in the field with her, sleeping on the threshing floor, observing the activity by the city gate, noticing her kinsman-redeemer and beautiful story of redemption.

Through Ruth, may you also begin to notice your story; your Kinsman-Redeemer, every believer's Kinsman-Redeemer: JESUS, who was also writing the lost world's story of redemption so long ago in the harvest fields, in that little village of Bethlehem.

Explanation of P.R.A.Y.

P. R.A.Y. is a tool and format we will use throughout our study which helps us focus on hearing God's voice as we pray, read, and listen.

> **P** – A time of PAUSE, breathing in and out as we calm our bodies, settling into a space of purposeful alone time with God, preparing to hear His voice.

> **R** – A time to REFLECT on God's Word as we read and perhaps re-read shorter passages of Scripture, trusting the Holy Spirit to draw our attention to any words or phrases that God could be using to speak to us.

> **A** – We ASK God in prayer to draw our attention to anything we need to say to Him or anything we need to hear from Him. This can be a time to confess any known or unknown sin, thanking Jesus for His forgiveness and help, OR also a time to ASK Jesus through prayerful petitions for help for others, our families, our world, and ourselves.

> **Y** – A time of YIELDING in prayer to the mission of Christ, tuning our hearts and our minds to hear and follow Jesus' instructions; a time of stillness as we YIELD to the promptings of the Holy Spirit to act.

Gleanings from The Edge

The Edge section in this devotional offers helpful nuggets of information pertaining to Scripture and the study of Ruth.

As background, Ruth, a Moabite woman, was a foreigner in the land of Israel. Foreigners during that time were required to "glean" or pick up grain in the fields on the "corner" or "edge" of the landowner's property.

God commanded the Israelites:

> *"When you reap the harvest of your land, do not reap to the very edges of your field or gather the gleanings of your harvest. Leave them for the poor and for the foreigner residing among you. I am the LORD your God."* Leviticus 23:22

May God add to your understanding as you "glean from the edge."

2
Ruth 1:1–7

PAUSE

Jesus, thank you for your Word and thank you that through it you transform me, teaching me more about YOU, my own self, and others. Help me to calm my scattered senses even now as I breathe in and out, inviting your Holy Spirit to be the teacher. Open my eyes through the study of Ruth I pray. Help me to listen to you—looking upward, inward, and outward through anything you may want to show me. In your precious name I pray. Amen.

REFLECT

Please get comfy, grab your Bible and pen and maybe even your favorite hot or cold beverage and read Ruth 1:1–7. Before you read, ask the Holy Spirit to teach you and to draw your attention to what He might be saying to you.

Ruth 1:1–7

¹ In the days when the judges ruled, there was a famine in the land, and a man from Bethlehem in Judah, together with his wife and two sons, went to live for a while in the country of Moab. ² The man's name was Elimelech, his wife's name Naomi, and the names of his two sons were Mahlon and Kilion. They were Ephrathites from Bethlehem, Judah. And they went to Moab and lived there. ³ Now Elimelech, Naomi's husband, died, and she was left with her two sons. ⁴ They married Moabite women, one named Orpah and the other Ruth. After they had lived there about ten years, ⁵both Mahlon and Kilion also died, and Naomi was left without her two sons and her husband. ⁶ When she heard in Moab that the Lord had come to the aid of his people by providing food for them, Naomi and her daughters-in-law prepared to return home from there. ⁷ With her two daughters-in-law she left the place where she had been living and set out on the road that would take them back to the land of Judah.

ASK

1. God, what are some words or thoughts in this passage that you see as important for me to pay attention to? Please help me notice.

2. Thinking back on our background and context for the book of Ruth, from verse 1, can you relate to any type of "chaos" or "famine" that you might be experiencing now, in recent days or even long ago?

3. From verses 1 and 2, what significance do you see in the writer sharing the specific details of the city, region, tribe, and names of the family fleeing to a foreign land trying to escape starvation?

4. Verses 3–5: New home, new land, enter new people—actually, new family members!!! AND, as if the first part of the journey wasn't challenging enough, it's now getting worse! Reflect on a time when you and your family may have been on the run from looming disaster, only to enter into more chaos once you settled into the new location or assignment. Write your answer here.

5. In verses 6 and 7, word reaches Naomi, who is still living in Moab, that provision from the Lord had come. Thinking back on question 1 and 4, are you able to name any provision(s) that the Lord provided for you and your family in the middle of the chaos you were in? Thank Him for it as you record your answer here.

YIELD

Jesus, from today's Scripture reading, is there anything you may be asking me to pay attention to in my own life that would require me to yield?

- Is there someone experiencing chaos that I need to help?

- Is there someone who caused my/our chaos that I need to forgive?

- What are you providing for us in our chaos that I cannot and may be even refusing to see as provision that has come from your hand?

Help me Jesus to YIELD and to TRUST you.

THE EDGE

As we spend time with God, it's important to recognize that the Holy Trinity is present and active in every believer. Our three in one, Triune God provides all we need for life and godliness (2 Peter 1:3). His voice and instructions are available to us through the reading of His Word and through the Holy Spirit.

The Holy Spirit helps us understand God's Word.

Nevertheless I tell you the truth. It is to your advantage that I go away; for if I do not go away, the Helper will not come to you; but if I depart, I will send Him to you. John 16:7 *(NKJV)*

God's Word is our road map in navigating life and in understanding God's heart. His Word IS His heart.

All Scripture is God-breathed and is useful for teaching, rebuking, correcting and training in righteousness, so that the man of God may be thoroughly equipped for every good work. 2 Timothy 3:16-17 *(NIV)*

Prayers & Reflections

3
Ruth 1:8–14

PAUSE

Lord Jesus, thank you for the gift of slowing down to spend time with you. I pause now, asking you to calm my scattered senses. Help me to breathe in and breathe out and to feel your presence—to focus on and become aware of the very presence of God. Use this time, Lord Jesus, to teach me. Teach me more about you and teach me more about myself and others. I am listening.

Help me to put aside the cares and worries of today and the things of yesterday and tomorrow that are out of my control. Help me to focus on simply being with you right now.

I am asking you, through your Holy Spirit, to speak to me through the study of Ruth and to draw my attention to anything you might be saying as I open your Word. I love you, Jesus. Amen.

REFLECT

In your most comfortable spot with your Bible and pen, ask the Holy Spirit to be your teacher as you read today's Scripture passage. Particularly listen for any words or phrases that stand out to you that God may be using to speak to your heart.

Ruth 1:8–14

8 Then Naomi said to her two daughters-in-law, "Go back, each of you, to your mother's home. May the Lord show kindness to you, as you have shown to your dead and to me. 9 May the Lord grant that each of you will find rest in the home of another husband." Then she kissed them and they wept aloud 10 and said to her, "We will go back with you to your people." 11 But Naomi said, "Return home, my daughters. Why would you come with me? Am I going to have any more sons, who could become your husbands? 12 Return home, my daughters; I am too old to have another husband. Even if I thought there was still hope for me—even if I had a husband tonight, and then gave birth to sons— [13] *would you wait until they grew up? Would you remain unmarried for them? No, my daughters. It is more bitter for me than for you, because the Lord's hand has gone out against me!"* [14] *At this they wept again. Then Orpah kissed her mother-in-law good-bye, but Ruth clung to her.*

ASK

1. Leaving a place of pain and heading to a place of hopeful "healing" can be risky. The path can be filled with threats! Ruth, Naomi, and Orpah were traveling on the Jericho Road (v.7) where robberies were not uncommon. (see comment in The Edge). What are you noticing right now regarding your current path? Take time to notice and journal. Are you experiencing feelings of fear, safety, joy, sorrow, curiosity, regret, etc? Talk to Jesus about your current path. Share with Him any and all concerns, asking Him to speak to you regarding your concerns.

2. Naomi, at this point, could see a hopeful future for her two daughter-in-laws, but not for herself. Why do you think we can often hold out hope for others, but not for ourselves? Write your answer. Reflect.

3. From today's verses, in her trauma and pain Naomi clearly "had her future mapped out" with an outcome she had predetermined! Could you get honest with God right now and confess to Him narratives that you thought you clearly had "mapped out" but may be noticing "His plan" unfolding?

4. Orpah returned back to Moab, but Ruth clung to Naomi. What Christ-like characteristics do you notice in Ruth? Be specific as you reflect on her backstory.

YIELD

Jesus, from today's Scripture reading, is there anything you may be asking me to pay attention to in my own life that would require me to yield?

- Is there anyone around me (in my family, neighborhood, or community) who is on an "uncertain road" that I need to extend the hand of kindness and friendship to today? Help me hear your voice and obey.

- What steps of faith do I need to take to help me stop "mapping out and anticipating my own outcomes" instead of waiting on you and trusting your outcomes?

- What steps of faith do I need to take to potentially get on "the road" you are asking me to get on?

- What narratives do I need help in—an "ask" of the Holy Spirit to disrupt my ideas and conclusions that "the Lord's hand has gone out against me"?

Help me Jesus to YIELD and to TRUST you.

> ## THE EDGE
>
> The Jericho Road is a 17-mile road that connects Jerusalem to Jericho. The road drops 3,600 feet in those 17 miles. It is a steep, winding, descending, remote road that for centuries has been a place of robberies and sufferings. The road is also known as "The Way of Blood" because of the danger that loomed on the road throughout history. The Jericho Road is the road Naomi and Ruth would have traveled on returning to Bethlehem from Moab.
>
> In Luke 10:25–37, Jesus referenced the Jericho Road when he told the parable of the Good Samaritan.

Prayer: The Road of Uncertainty

Lead me Lord,
into the reassurance of Your Presence.
I come to You, precious Savior,
to remind me that
Your power is made perfect
in weakness.
On the Road of Uncertainty
Ruth chose YOU, Father!
The God of Naomi!
It wasn't Naomi's beauty and riches
that drew Ruth to her God,
it was her faithfulness
despite enormous loss.
In my loss,
in my sorrow,
Grant me the grace to hear your voice
and feel your nearness.
You are a compassionate God
Who provides bread
in time of famine.
You are a merciful God
Who covers in blessing
through seasons that are barren.
You are a loving God
Who fills with JOY
and overcomes sorrow.
May You find me FAITHFUL
when walking

on the Road of Uncertainty.
Teach me Your way, Lord.
Lead me on the straight path.
Graciously grow in me
wisdom and courage
through hardship
and uncertainty.
As I draw near,
reassure me
in TRUTH
that security is found in You alone.
In returning to You,
resting in You,
saving grace is realized.
In quietness and TRUST
I am made strong.
In the powerful name
of my Lord Jesus.
Amen.

Prayers & Reflections

4
Ruth 1:15–22

PAUSE

Lord Jesus, I praise you for your presence and promise that you never leave me or forsake me. You are here. Thank you for your love and grace that holds me together minute by minute. Help me now to breathe in and breathe out calmly, resting and pausing in the presence of God as I anticipate what you will teach me through your Word. I welcome you Holy Spirit to be my teacher today as I study Ruth. Have your way in me Lord Jesus, cleanse me from any and all distractions, helping me to focus my scattered senses onto you. Amen.

REFLECT

In your most comfortable spot with your Bible and pen, ask the Holy Spirit to be your teacher as you read today's Scripture passage. Particularly listen for any words or phrases that stand out to you that God may be using to speak to your heart.

Ruth 1:15–22

[15]*"Look," said Naomi, "your sister-in-law is going back to her people and her gods. Go back with her."* [16]*But Ruth replied, "Don't urge me to leave you or to turn back from you. Where you go I will go, and where you stay I will stay. Your people will be my people and your God my God.* [17]*Where you die I will die, and there I will be buried. May the Lord deal with me, be it ever so severely, if anything but death separates you and me."* [18]*When Naomi realised that Ruth was determined to go with her, she stopped urging her.* [19]*So the two women went on until they came to Bethlehem. When they arrived in Bethlehem, the whole town was stirred because of them, and the women exclaimed, "Can this be Naomi?"* [20]*"Don't call me, Naomi," she told them. "Call me Mara, because the Almighty has made my life very bitter.* [21]*I went away full, but the Lord has brought me back empty. Why call me Naomi? The Lord has afflicted me; the Almighty has brought misfortune upon me."* [22]*So*

Naomi returned from Moab accompanied by Ruth the Moabitess, her daughter-in-law, arriving in Bethlehem as the barley harvest was beginning.

ASK

1. Verses 16–17: Ruth's decision was firm. In a historical moment on the Jericho Road, Ruth chose a new identity—new family, new town, (new) God, new people group, even pre-deciding to adopt the burial traditions of the Israelites! What has God used in your life (moves, new places, new faces, new traditions, etc.) to help form and reshape your identity? Be specific.

2. Naomi, apparently unrecognizable, was now returning from Moab to Bethlehem (see The Edge). She had become very bitter, blaming God. What in your life has happened or not happened where you might be tempted to say like Naomi, "the Almighty has made my life very bitter"? Turn this into a conversation with God in prayer or in writing, asking Jesus to give you His perspective.

3. Verse 22 is loaded with meaning (see The Edge). In the bleakest of moments, God always sends an "as the barley harvest was beginning" signal of hope. What "barley harvest" (big or small) has come your way lately?

YIELD

Jesus, from today's Scripture reading, is there anything you may be asking me to pay attention to in my own life that would require me to yield?

- Jesus, what new or old evidences of YOUR identity being formed in me, would you like me to stop, notice, and thank you for?
- Naomi's God became Ruth's God. Is there anyone in my life, Lord, that I need to share YOU with today?
- Is there anything OLD (like Moab), or anything NEW (like Bethlehem), that I need to let go of or embrace?

Help me Jesus to YIELD and to TRUST you.

THE EDGE

Some history and word meanings that may empower understanding in today's Scripture passage:

Naomi: Hebrew, meaning "pleasant; gentle" (compare this to Mara which means "bitter")

Ruth: Hebrew, meaning "compassionate friend"

Bethlehem: Hebrew, meaning "House of Bread"

Judah: Hebrew, meaning "Praise"

History of Moab: A people group that started in Genesis 19:30–38, as a result of Lot's incestuous encounter with his two daughters. (Lot was Abraham's nephew.) Lot's older daughter gave birth to a son who she named Moab (the Moabites of today), and the younger daughter gave birth to a son she named Ben-Ammi (the Ammonites of today)—both enemies of Israel.

Prayers & Reflections

5
Ruth 2:1–7

PAUSE

Lord Jesus, I pause before you now, breathing in and out, asking you to calm my scattered senses, reflecting on the very presence of God. Please remove any distractions from me, helping me to focus on you as I long to hear your voice. Please remove from me all anxieties, Jesus, and help me to confess any sin or anything known or unknown that is creating distance between us. Thank you that you forgive me and thank you that you never leave or forsake me. I center my attention on you now, asking you to speak to me through the study of your Word. Amen.

REFLECT

In your most comfortable spot with your Bible and pen, ask the Holy Spirit to be your teacher as you read today's Scripture passage. Particularly listen for any words or phrases that stand out to you that God may be using to speak to your heart.

Ruth 2:1–7

¹Now Naomi had a relative on her husband's side, from the clan of Elimelech, a man of standing, whose name was Boaz. ²And Ruth the Moabitess said to Naomi, "Let me go to the fields and pick up the leftover grain behind anyone in whose eyes I find favour." Naomi said to her, "Go ahead, my daughter." ³So she went out and began to glean in the fields behind the harvesters. As it turned out, she found herself working in a field belonging to Boaz, who was from the clan of Elimelech. ⁴Just then Boaz arrived from Bethlehem and greeted the harvesters, "The Lord be with you!" "The Lord bless you!" they called back. ⁵Boaz asked the foreman of his harvesters, "Whose young woman is that?" ⁶The foreman replied, "She is the Moabitess who came back from Moab with Naomi. ⁷She said, 'Please let me glean and gather among the sheaves behind the harvesters.' She went into the field and has worked steadily from morning till now, except for a short rest in the shelter."

ASK

1. In poverty, now a cultural outcast and young widow living in a foreign land, Ruth decides to dig in and get to work. Where has God asked you to "dig in" lately where, like Ruth, you may feel like a foreigner picking up leftovers? Talk to God about that in prayer or by writing your response.

2. Verse 3 is a very big deal! Ruth ends up in Boaz's field. Some versions say "As it turned out," and other versions say "And her hap was to light on a part of the field belonging to Boaz." This is the same as saying "It just so happened." When have you noticed your natural choices being an "It just so happened moment" where hindsight teaches you that God's incredible provision and protection were in it?

3. Reread verses 4 and 5. What do you notice about Boaz's character in these verses?

4. What do you notice about Ruth's character from verses 6 and 7?

YIELD

Jesus, from today's Scripture reading, is there anything you may be asking me to pay attention to in my own life that would require me to yield?

- Is there someone in my family, neighborhood, or community who, like Ruth, is laboring as a "foreigner, gleaning scraps"? If so Jesus, do you desire for me to help? If so, how?

- Jesus, help me to notice any big or little decision I'm facing right now that you may be asking me to trust my instincts and YOUR sovereignty? (See sovereign definition in The Edge.)

- Are there any character traits YOU are asking me to grow in or display in my workplace or in my home that would honor YOU and serve as a witness to others of YOUR excellence at work in me?

Help me Jesus to YIELD and to TRUST you.

THE EDGE

The Scripture below explains the Mosaic Law regarding foreigners' boundaries for "gleaning in the fields."

"When you reap the harvest of your land, do not reap to the very edges of your field or gather the gleanings of your harvest. Do not go over your vineyard a second time or pick up the grapes that have fallen. Leave them for the poor and the foreigner. I am the Lord your God."
Leviticus 19:9–10

Sovereign: rule, dominion, absolute mastery over

Prayers & Reflections

6
Ruth 2:8–14

PAUSE

Lord Jesus, I come before you now, ready and eager to hear your voice. I long to feel your presence. I pray that you will calm my scattered senses, as I breathe in and out, focusing on the very presence of God. Thank you, that you are my sun and shield; you disinfect and cleanse my soul and you also shield my soul from things that bring me harm. Help me today to hear your voice, your tender sweet voice, as I read from the book of Ruth. Help me to know you are near and to trust you, Jesus. Amen.

REFLECT

In your most comfortable spot with your Bible and pen, ask the Holy Spirit to be your teacher as you read today's Scripture passage. Particularly listen for any words or phrases that stand out to you that God may be using to speak to your heart.

Ruth 2:8–14

8So Boaz said to Ruth, "My daughter, listen to me. Don't go and glean in another field and don't go away from here. Stay here with my servant girls. 9Watch the field where the men are harvesting, and follow along after the girls. I have told the men not to touch you. And whenever you are thirsty, go and get a drink from the water jars the men have filled." 10At this, she bowed down with her face to the ground. She exclaimed, "Why have I found such favour in your eyes that you notice me—a foreigner?" 11Boaz replied, "I've been told all about what you have done for your mother-in-law since the death of your husband—how you left your father and mother and your homeland and came to live with a people you did not know before. 12May the Lord repay you for what you have done. May you be richly rewarded by the Lord for what you have done. May you be richly rewarded by the Lord, the God of Israel, under whose wings you have come to take refuge." 13"May I continue to find favour in your eyes, my lord," she said. "You have given me comfort and have spoken kindly to your servant—though I do not have the standing of one of your servant girls." [14] At mealtime Boaz said to her, "Come over here. Have some bread and dip it in the wine vinegar." When she sat down with the harvesters, he offered her some roasted grain. She ate all she wanted and had some left over.

ASK

1. Reflecting back on the introduction for the book of Ruth, with the lineage of Christ unfolding in each chapter, what characteristics of Jesus do you notice in Boaz in verses 8–14? In Ruth?

2. What characteristics of Jesus do you notice in your life? Record these and thank Him!

3. What specifically does Boaz offer Ruth that Christ offers us?

4. In verse 14, we see Ruth the foreigner sitting at the landowner's table where "leftover grain" has taken on a whole new meaning. What hypothetical or real "table" have you sat at recently and left feeling satisfied, even having "leftovers."

5. Can you think of a time in your journey, past or present, where "picking up scraps" for survival has now become something you give away as a blessing to others? OR, when you were on the road of uncertainty, only now to find yourself "taking refuge" under the wings of the God of Israel? Please share.

YIELD

Jesus, from today's Scripture reading, is there anything you may be asking me to pay attention to in my own life that would require me to yield?

- Is there an area in my life in any form, Jesus, where pride is creating in me "attitudes" that are robbing me of the blessings of being at "the table," even as a foreigner? Help me confess that now and repent.

- Is there any area in my life, Lord Jesus, where unforgiveness and bitterness is robbing me of a place at the table, even as a foreigner?

- Jesus, is there anyone I need to welcome to my table?

- Jesus, is there any table you're asking me to sit down at where I'm refusing?

Help me Jesus to YIELD and to TRUST you.

THE EDGE

Much like crossing the U.S. southern border today where women and children are at risk for safety, Ruth, a Moabite coming into Bethlehem, would have been at risk working in a field as a young woman without a protector.

Reflect on Matthew 26:17–30, "The Last Supper," when Jesus dipped His bread and the significance of that bread, as you ponder Boaz's invitation for Ruth to dip her bread while in Bethlehem, "The House of Bread."

Prayer: Field of Harvest

I open the windows of my heart
and soul to YOU Lord Jesus;
fill me with the goodness
of Your Light, Your Love.
May Your face shine upon me,
enlightening every ounce of my being!
Holy Spirit,
open my eyes to see,
my ears to hear;
Help my mind to perceive
and understand.
Grant me a heart that responds.
Thank You for everything in my life
that requires me to run to You;
For the refuge arranged by YOU
offering the protection
and provision needed
under the shadow of Your wing.
Guide me Lord,
be my tender shepherd.
Counsel me Lord, be my wise teacher.
Forgive me Lord, change and rearrange
the stubborn places in my heart,
turning my dry deserts
into springs of JOY.
Refine me Lord, cultivate in me
a heart of praise!
Create in me blind trust
like Naomi,
Who leaned into You

through devastation.
Equip me with loyalty
like Ruth, who was faithful
through the unknown.
May I love and embody
compassion for others like Boaz,
recognizing the kindness of others
toward me.
For You form the hearts of ALL
and consider everything we do.
You have blessed me, Father,
with the full reward
of knowing Jesus,
just as Boaz blessed Ruth.
May I harvest gratefully
in the righteous fields
of knowing Jesus,
sharing His abundance
with everyone I meet.
In the gift of Jesus I pray.
Amen.

Prayers & Reflections

7
Ruth 2:15–23

PAUSE

Breathe in slowly and breathe out, pausing in the presence of the Lord.

Use the space below to write out a prayer to God.

REFLECT

In your most comfortable spot with your Bible and pen, ask the Holy Spirit to be your teacher as you read today's Scripture passage. Particularly listen for any words or phrases that stand out to you that God may be using to speak to your heart.

Ruth 2:15–23

[15]As she got up to glean, Boaz gave orders to his men, "Even if she gathers among the sheaves, don't embarrass her. [16]Rather, pull out some stalks for her from the bundles and leave them for her to pick up, and don't rebuke her." [17]So Ruth gleaned in the field until evening. Then she threshed the barley she had gathered, and it amounted to about an ephah. [18]She carried it back to town, and her mother-in-law saw how much she had gathered. Ruth also brought out and gave her what she had left over after she had eaten enough. Her mother-in-law asked her, "Where did you glean today? Where did you work? [19]Blessed be the man who took notice of you!" Then Ruth told her mother-in-law about the one at whose place she had been working. "The name of the man I worked with today is Boaz," she said. [20]"The Lord bless him!" Naomi said to her daughter-in-law. "He has not stopped showing his kindness to the living and the dead." She added, "That man is our close relative; he is one of our kinsman-redeemers." [21]Then Ruth the Moabitess said, "He even said to me 'Stay with my workers until they finish harvesting all my grain.'" [22]Naomi said to Ruth her daughter-in-law, "It will be good for you, my daughter, to go with his girls, because in someone else's field you might be harmed." [23]So Ruth stayed close to the servant girls of Boaz to glean until the barley and wheat harvests were finished. And she lived with her mother-in-law.

ASK

1. In these verses, Boaz's empathy and protection of Ruth in her vulnerability foreshadows what we know to be true about the heart of Jesus. Can you

recall a time when, like Ruth, you felt the strong presence of Jesus looking out for you during a season of vulnerability? Please share.

2. Ruth's character—honesty, loyalty, and hard work—jump off the page in today's Scripture reading. Why do you think the author included "Ruth also brought out and gave her what she had left over after she had eaten enough," in this passage? Reflect on these qualities and share what you believe God thinks about them.

3. In today's passage, we're beginning to see the incredible significance of verse 22, Chapter 1, "as the barley harvest was beginning." Ruth had traveled an "uncertain road," just so hap to land in a "field of hope" and now was postured to meet her kinsman-redeemer (see definition below). What are you noticing in Ruth's story and/or in your story that begs the question "Could God be doing something special in the midst of impossible?"

4. Today's passage ends with the incredible display of humility in the life of Ruth (working alongside Boaz's servant girls, gleaning in the harvest field until finished, and living with her mother-in-law). What has God asked you to do lately that has humbled you? Could you look up a verse in your Bible (concordance in the back or google it) that talks about what God thinks about humility? Please record the verse here.

5. Can you think of a time in your journey, past or present, where "picking up scraps" for survival has now become something you give away as a blessing to others? OR, when you were on the road of uncertainty, only now to find yourself "taking refuge" under the wings of the God of Israel? Please share.

YIELD

Jesus, from today's Scripture reading, is there anything you may be asking me to pay attention to in my own life that would require me to yield?

- Where in my life, Jesus, am I practicing humility? Help me to recognize this as a gift from you.

- Where, Jesus, in my life am I behaving pridefully?

- Is there anything you're asking me to do that would help me become more humble?

- Is there a hidden attitude of pride in my heart that I'm making excuses for (calling it something else), when you might actually be saying "This is pride"?

- Is there someone I need to confront and seek conflict resolution (either me or them), where pride has been the crux of the problem?

- Jesus, can you please teach me at a personal level what it means to be humble?

Help me Jesus to YIELD and to TRUST you.

THE EDGE

Definitions that will add meaning to today's reading:

Glean: to collect bit by bit (particularity after a harvest season)

Sheaves: a bundle of grain stalks laid lengthwise and tied together

Threshing: the process of separating the grain from the rest of the plant (the chaff)

Ephah: measurement equaling 22 liters

Kinsman-Redeemer: a male relative who has the responsibility to help a relative in need or danger, particularly during the historical period in the Old Testament

Harvest Season: lasted about 90–100 days and followed the maturation of the wheat and barley crops

Prayers & Reflections

8
Ruth 3:1-6

PAUSE

Lord Jesus, I pause before you now, seeking to calm in your presence and to hear your voice. There is no sweeter voice than yours. I breathe in and breathe out, seeking stillness as I focus on the very presence of God.

Thank you for the study of Ruth. Thank you for all you are teaching me through the life and journey of this Moabite woman. Help me to hear your voice and to listen to anything and everything you may want me to know and understand as I read today's verses. Thank you for being a very "hands on" God who is interested in every detail of my life. Thank you for being my Redeemer and my very rich Reward. Amen.

REFLECT

In your most comfortable spot with your Bible and pen, ask the Holy Spirit to be your teacher as you read today's Scripture passage. Particularly listen for any words or phrases that stand out to you that God may be using to speak to your heart.

Ruth 3:1-6

¹*One day Naomi her mother-in-law said to her, "My daughter, should I not try to find a home for you, where you will be well provided for? ²Is not Boaz, with whose servant girls you have been, a kinsman of ours? Tonight he will be winnowing barley on the threshing-floor. ³Wash and perfume yourself, and put on your best clothes. Then go down to the threshing-floor, but don't let him know you are there until he has finished eating and drinking. ⁴When he lies down, note the place where he is lying. Then go and uncover his feet and lie down. He will tell you what to do."*

⁵*"I will do whatever you say," Ruth answered. ⁶So she went down to the threshing-floor and did everything her mother-in-law told her to do.*

ASK

1. At the start of Ruth 3, we are given two words: "One day…" Time has passed and Ruth is now being referred to as "daughter" rather than "daughter-in-law," with words of endearment by Naomi. Please share how you may be noticing an "identity change" as God continues to write your story with the passage of time.

2. What "endearing words" has God spoken to you lately that you are now able to hear, that maybe you could not hear before? What specifically does Boaz offer Ruth that Christ offers us?

3. Notice and record the practical advice or "tips" Naomi instructs Ruth to follow. What practical tip(s) has an older "Naomi" offered you in life, that has helped you become the woman God created you to be? What tip(s) could you now offer a younger "Ruth" that might empower a woman in becoming who God has made her to be?

4.   What attributes had to be in place in Ruth's heart for her to be able to say in verse 5, "I will do whatever you say." What attributes have to be in place in our heart to be able to say, "Lord, I will do whatever you say"? Please share.

YIELD

Jesus, from today's Scripture reading, is there anything you may be asking me to pay attention to in my own life that would require me to yield?

- Jesus, am I obedient to you? If not, why not?

- Jesus, is there any area in my heart where you have given me practical tips, and I am ignoring them?

- Jesus, is there anyone in my life that you desire me to mentor like Naomi mentored Ruth?

- Jesus, is there anyone in my life, like a Naomi, who you would like to mentor me, even if I have to approach them with an ask?

Help me Jesus to YIELD and to TRUST you.

THE EDGE

In today's verses, we see an interesting cultural account of a woman laying horizontally at a man's feet on the threshing floor during the harvest season. Though these verses can be interpreted many different ways, research indicates that this was a cultural behavior signaling to a young man that a woman desired to be protected and provided for by him.

Prayers & Reflections

9
Ruth 3:7–13

PAUSE

Lord Jesus, I pause before you now, longing to hear your voice and desiring to notice your nearness. As I breathe in and out, calm my scattered senses, helping me to focus on the very presence of God.

Speak to me Lord Jesus, and cleanse me from any sin known or unknown.

Help me to openly confess to you anything within or without, that is contrary to your character or your will. Create in me a desire to follow you with my whole heart and to obey you immediately and completely. I love you Jesus and I long to be with you. Speak to me now, your servant is listening. Amen.

REFLECT

In your most comfortable spot with your Bible and pen, ask the Holy Spirit to be your teacher as you read today's Scripture passage. Particularly listen for any words or phrases that stand out to you that God may be using to speak to your heart.

Ruth 3:7–13

7When Boaz had finished eating and drinking and was in good spirits, he went over to lie down at the far end of the grain pile. Ruth approached quietly, uncovered his feet and lay down. 8 In the middle of the night something startled the man, and he turned and discovered a woman lying at his feet.

9"Who are you?" he asked.

"I am your servant Ruth," she said. "Spread the corner of your garment over me, since you are a kinsman-redeemer."

10"The Lord bless you, my daughter," he replied. "This kindness is greater than that which you showed earlier: You have not run after the younger men, whether rich or poor. 11And now, my daughter, don't be afraid. I will do for you all you ask. All my fellow townsmen know that you are a woman of noble character. [12]Although it is true that I am near of kin, there is a kinsman- redeemer nearer than I. [13]Stay here for the night, and in the morning if he wants to redeem, good; let him redeem. But if he is not willing, as surely as the Lord lives I will do it. Lie here until morning."

ASK

1. Trust and submission. In today's verses, in a land unknown, Ruth is following the lead of another, letting go of control and trusting her outcomes to Naomi's instructions and the God of Israel. In your "land of the unknown," what is God asking you to let go of and to give up control of?

2. In your "land of the unknown," what steps of trust is God asking you to take?

3. In today's verses, God is at work behind the scenes in ways that we won't fully understand until the end of the story. Is there anything that you notice God doing, past or present, that causes you to ponder His movement in arranging your future story?

4. In Ruth's "Unknown Land," Boaz is intent on finding her the right kinsman-redeemer, even if it's himself. What attributes of Jesus do you see foreshadowed here in Boaz?

5. What stood out to you in today's lesson that may have been "God's whisper to you," or His voice speaking to you?

YIELD

Jesus, from today's Scripture reading, is there anything you may be asking me to pay attention to in my own life that would require me to yield?

- Jesus, are there any specific, personal invitations for me today from our reading in which you are inviting me to "yield"? I long to hear and see.

- Is there any tradition of another that I have viewed judgmentally or critically without knowing the cultural context? Help me to be honest with you Jesus, and to confess anything that is offensive to you or others. Help me to see others with your eyes. I need your guidance and truth.

- Jesus, what plan or steps do I need to take to help any "spiritual foreigner" I may know meet YOU, the true Kinsman-Redeemer?

Help me Jesus to YIELD and to TRUST you.

THE EDGE

In Ruth 3:9 the word *garment* appears as *wing, covering*, and *cloak* in other translations. The Hebrew word here is *kanaph*, which means "an edge or extremity; specifically (of a bird or army), a wing (of a garment or bed-clothing), a flap, corner."

In Ezekiel 16:8, the prophet speaking God's words to the wayward nation of Israel, delivers the following:

> *Later I passed by, and when I looked at you and saw that you were old enough for love, I spread the corner of my garment over you and covered your nakedness. I gave you my solemn oath and entered into a covenant with you, declares the Sovereign LORD, and you became mine.*

The same Hebrew word *kanaph* in Ruth 3:9, "spread the corner of your garment over me," (kinsman-redeemer/marriage), is also used in Ezekiel 16:8 by God Himself, "I spread the corner of my garment over you," (Kinsman-Redeemer, Jesus/marriage). Receive these kisses God is blowing from heaven!

Prayer: Floor of Faith

*Father, forgive me when I ask You
for the easy life.
May I instead stand firm
on the Floor of Faithfulness,
surrendering to Your wise ways;
to Your plans of growth and goodness.
Teach me Lord Jesus to trust You!
Your desire is for me to be faithful
through all things.
May I catch a glimpse
of the deep and mysterious truths
that flow from the things
You allow in my life.
May I sing
in the Shadow of Your Wings!
For there is abundant JOY
in Your Presence;
there is comfort and protection
found in Your Love.
May I find HOPE in Truth past,
in present blessings,
in Your promises,
in Your faithfulness,
in Your grace,
just like Ruth.
Transform my life, Lord.
Guard me from the traps of sin,
self-pity, bitterness, self-centeredness,
and all things that rob me of YOU.
May I instead, in the humility of Jesus,*

*trust in Your Sovereign will;
follow the movement
of Your compassionate Hand,
so that I may too, like Boaz,
be an instrument of provision for
others.
May Your character of loving-
kindness
flow from my heart.
May my life reflect
a worshipful lifestyle
as I stand steadfast
on the Floor of Faith,
praising You for the abundant life
You offer as I overcome,
and embrace the PEACE
that is mine in Your Presence.
In the Faithfulness of Jesus I pray.
AMEN.*

Prayers & Reflections

10
Ruth 3:14–18

PAUSE

Lord Jesus, I pause before you now, breathing in and out, desiring peace in your presence as you calm my scattered senses. Help me to slow down and be fully present. I am listening for your voice. Speak to me now Jesus through your Holy Spirit, and help me to gaze upon your beauty as I ponder who YOU are and who I am as your child. Help me to notice all the ways you are providing and protecting, even when my eyes can't see. Jesus, turn my heart into a land of plenty—a landscape where thankfulness and gratitude abound, removing the rocky soil and spiritual drought that has robbed me for way too long. Open my eyes to see and my ears to hear and my senses to be awakened to every movement of you Jesus, my Kinsman-Redeemer. Amen.

REFLECT

In your most comfortable spot with your Bible and pen, ask the Holy Spirit to be your teacher as you read today's Scripture passage. Particularly listen for any words or phrases that stand out to you that God may be using to speak to your heart.

Ruth 3:14–18

14So she lay at his feet until morning, but got up before anyone could be recognised; and he said, "Don't let it be known that a woman came to the threshing-floor."

15He also said, "Bring me the shawl you are wearing and hold it out." When she did so, he poured into it six measures of barley and put it on her. Then he went back to town.

16When Ruth came to her mother-in-law, Naomi asked, "How did it go, my daughter?" Then she told her everything Boaz had done for her 17and added, "He gave me these six measures of barley, saying, `Don't go back to your mother-in-law empty-handed.'"

18Then Naomi said, "Wait, my daughter, until you find out what happens. For the man will not rest until the matter is settled today."

ASK

1. From verse 14, Ruth continues to submit and wait in a cultural paradigm modeling trust in a land unknown. What are you noticing in your life where "submitting and waiting" is becoming increasingly hard (like laying on a wooden floor), but you see God's hand in it? Ask Jesus to speak to you, giving you clarity about your hard space and His purpose in it.

2. From today's verses, we see Boaz noticing Ruth's shawl and providing for her (and Naomi) rather than taking advantage of her. How has God surprised you recently by noticing what you have and making "provision" for you, when you may have felt vulnerable and afraid, anticipating that someone might be positioned to "take" from you? Thank Him.

3. What has God "filled" your hands/home with, not leaving you "empty handed"? Could you write down 5–10 blessings that have come from His hand? Thank Him.

4. In verse 18, the former "Mara" (Naomi) is now receiving a renewed vision of "HOPE" in the God of Israel. (Remember formerly she had announced that The Almighty had brought her back "empty," Ruth 1:21). Can you be specific about a time, past or present, when your hands were completely "empty" but the God of Israel surprised you by filling your shawl with six measures of barley?

YIELD

Jesus, from today's Scripture reading, is there anything you may be asking me to pay attention to in my own life that would require me to yield?

- Jesus, do I need to work on my heart attitude of thankfulness? Better stated... Jesus, am I ungrateful? Jesus, give me eyes to see and a heart that understands the blessings of a thankful heart.

- Jesus, help me recall a time when my heart was filled with gratitude for what you did. Help me celebrate that again, even now!

- Jesus, am I missing any of your provisions because my eyes are clouded with a lens of criticism and complaining?

- Jesus, open my eyes to see all the ways you are working to turn any of my dire situations into stories of redemption.

- Jesus, is there anyone in my life whose shawl I need to dump six measures of barley into today? Show me and help me to obey.

Help me Jesus to YIELD and to TRUST you.

THE EDGE

Six measures of barley = approx. 2.5 gallons

Significance of barley: it was a "first fruit" of the harvest

Jesus is our first fruit from the dead—our resurrected King (1 Corinthians 15:20–23)

Note: Ruth "waiting"at the feet of Boaz has strong semblance to us as "believers" waiting at the feet of Jesus.

Prayers & Reflections

11
Ruth 4:1–12

PAUSE

Lord Jesus, my Kinsman-Redeemer, I pause before you now asking you to quiet my body, soul, and spirit. As I breathe in and breathe out, I pray your Holy Spirit would cover me and envelop me with the peace of your presence, helping me know you are near. Today, as I begin to read the last chapter of Ruth, open my eyes, Holy Trinity, to see your authority and Kingship over the past, the present, and the future. Help me to notice your authority and to submit to your Lordship over my life—past, present, and future and over all my circumstances. Open my eyes and heart to see the evidence of YOU having been there all along, and all the ways you are working in every situation—past, present, and future—to redeem all things. I love you, Jesus. I welcome your redemptive plan in my life, including all things that were planned by you so long ago; things that transpired and things that were thrown off course by sin, the world, and the enemy. Perform your work of redemption now I pray, Lord Jesus. Have your way in me. In your precious, timeless, and matchless name I ask these things. Amen.

REFLECT

In your most comfortable spot with your Bible and pen, ask the Holy Spirit to be your teacher as you read today's Scripture passage. Particularly listen for any words or phrases that stand out to you that God may be using to speak to your heart.

Ruth 4:1–12

¹Meanwhile Boaz went up to the town gate and sat there. When the kinsman-redeemer he had mentioned came along, Boaz said, "Come over here, my friend, and sit down." So he went over and sat down.

²Boaz took ten of the elders of the town and said, "Sit here," and they did so. ³Then he said to the kinsman-redeemer, "Naomi, who has come back from Moab, is selling the piece of land that belonged to our brother Elimelech. ⁴I thought I should bring the matter to your attention and suggest that you buy it in the presence of these seated here and in the presence of the elders of my people. If you will redeem it, do so. But if you will not, tell me, so I will know. For no-one has the right to do it except you, and I am next in line."

"I will redeem it," he said.

⁵ Then Boaz said, "On the day you buy the land from Naomi and from Ruth the Moabitess, you acquire the dead man's widow, in order to maintain the name of the dead with his property."

⁶ At this, the kinsman-redeemer said, "Then I cannot redeem it because I might endanger my own estate. You redeem it yourself. I cannot do it."

⁷ (Now in earlier times in Israel, for the redemption and transfer of property to become final, one party took off his sandal and gave it to the other. This was the method of legalising transactions in Israel.)

⁸ So the kinsman-redeemer said to Boaz, "Buy it yourself." And he removed his sandal.

⁹ Then Boaz announced to the elders and all the people, "Today you are witnesses that I have bought from Naomi all the property of Elimelech, Kilion and Mahlon. ¹⁰ I have also acquired Ruth the Moabitess, Mahlon's widow, as my wife, in order to maintain the name of the dead with his property, so that his name will not disappear from among his family or from the town records. Today you are witnesses!"

¹¹ Then the elders and all those at the gate said, "We are witnesses. May the Lord make the woman who is coming into your home like Rachel and Leah, who together built up the house of Israel. May you have standing in Ephrathah and be famous in Bethlehem. 12 Through the offspring the Lord gives you by this young woman, may your family be like that of Perez, whom Tamar bore to Judah."

ASK

1. In today's opening verses, we see Boaz, man of strong character and tender patience, sitting by the town gate with ten town elders (see The Edge), desiring to establish Ruth's kinsman-redeemer. Acting in nobility (though it may have cost him his bride), why do you think the behavior of "honoring protocol/rules" matters to God? Without the oppression of legalism, do you see yourself as a rule/protocol follower? Why or why not?

2. What would have/could have happened to the lineage of Jesus (making its appearance here), if Boaz had ignored the proper protocol?

3. "Taking off your shoe" and giving it to another was an oath of honor between two negotiating parties during Biblical times. This very practice demonstrated vulnerability and principles of "grounded commitment." Can you recall a time in your life or in your experience with another when you left the negotiating scene knowing that honor had taken center stage because of the vulnerable and trustworthy act(s) of those present? Please share. (In today's cultural climate we can't hear enough of these encouragements!)

4. Two kinsman-redeemers are in the potential mix for Ruth in Chapter 4. One said "I cannot do it," the other said "I have also acquired Ruth the Moabitess…" In other words, "kinsman-redeemer accomplished!" Ponder the following: The Law of Moses (good behavior), can't redeem us (kind of like Boaz's next of kin)—only Christ can redeem us. What does this truth bring up in your heart as you think about what happened that day at Bethlehem's City Gate?

5. Long before the prophetic words of Micah 5:2 land on the pages of Scripture, the fulfillment of the "Greatest News" ever given to mankind (Jesus' coming), is unfolding at the City Gate in Ruth 4:9–11. Read Micah 5:2 and reread Ruth 4:9–11. Look for beautiful connections. Write down what God is showing you!

> But you, Bethlehem Ephrathah, though you are small among the clans
> of Judah, out of you will come for me one who will be ruler over Israel,
> whose origins are from of old, from ancient times.
>
> Micah 5:2 NIV (2011)

YIELD

Jesus, from today's Scripture reading, is there anything you may be asking me to pay attention to in my own life that would require me to yield?

- Jesus, there is so much here in Ruth 4:1–12. What are you asking me to pay attention to?

- Jesus, is there any particular thing in my own genealogy and family story that you would like for me to notice today? Is there anything/anyone you are redeeming and where is your redemptive work happening? Help me to notice.

- Jesus, do I need to confess to you any attitude in my heart, or any inner vow or decision I've made about myself or others, totally dismissing your ability to redeem the impossible? Help me to repent and to turn to YOU in trust.

- Jesus, help me to hear you and obey how I can be part of your redemptive plan in the lives of my family, my neighborhood, my community, the world, and myself.

Help me Jesus to YIELD and to TRUST you.

THE EDGE

The town or city gate in Biblical cultures was like today's modern courthouse. It was the location within a town where legal matters were settled, particularly land transactions, divorce, and marriage.

The number "ten" carries lots of varied meaning(s) in Hebrew culture. Ten elders at the town gate was significant for a "majority" to be established in a legal matter. It was also the number required for corporate Jewish worship to occur.

Deuteronomy 25:5–10 is a great reference for the Old Testament practice of "unsandaling."

Genesis 38 records the story of Tamar and Judah.

Matthew 2:6 is a New Testament reference to Micah 5:2.

Rachel and Leah (along with servants Zilpah and Bilah) between them gave birth to sons who eventually became the 12 tribes of Israel.

Bethlehem Ephrathah is the former ancient name of Bethlehem Judah.

Notice the connection in Ruth 4:12 to Jesus, "The Lion from the Tribe of Judah."

Notice the connection in Ruth 4 and the decisions at the city gate to the ultimate location of Jesus' birth.

Prayers & Reflections

12
Ruth 4:13–22

PAUSE

Jesus, I pause before you now, breathing in and out, asking you to calm my heart.
Help me to focus on your presence now, noticing anything you'd like to tell me or
show me, or maybe even enjoy just being STILL. I welcome your transformative power
in my life as I sit with you. Do what you will. As I read the last verses in the book of
Ruth, let not the world, my flesh, or the enemy rob me of the truths you desire me to
know. Plant deep within my heart the timeless principles of Ruth's reality—a woman
who trusted you in the impossible. Mold in me that same desire to trust and the
willingness to obey you no matter what. Use me, Lord Jesus, to love others without
conditions, that I may dwell in the peace of your presence, dealing out YOUR hope and
love to everyone I meet. You are the God of Ruth, you are the God of Hope, you are the
God of Love, you are the God of Life, you are the God of Me. Come, Lord Jesus, come.
Have your way. In your precious name I pray. Amen.

REFLECT

In your most comfortable spot with your Bible and pen, ask the Holy Spirit to be your
teacher as you read today's Scripture passage. Particularly listen for any words or
phrases that stand out to you that God may be using to speak to your heart.

Ruth 4:13–22

*13So Boaz took Ruth and she became his wife. Then he went to her, and the Lord
enabled her to conceive, and she gave birth to a son. 14The women said to Naomi:
"Praise be the Lord, who this day has not left you without a kinsman-redeemer.
May he become famous throughout Israel! 15He will renew your life and sustain you
in your old age. For your daughter-in-law, who loves you and who is better to you
than seven sons, has given him birth." 16Then Naomi took the child, laid him in her
lap and cared for him. 17The women living there said, "Naomi has a son." And they
named him Obed. He was the father of Jesse, the father of David.*

18This, then, is the family line of Perez: Perez was the father of Hezron, 19Hezron the father of Ram, Ram the father of Amminadab, 20Amminadab the father of Nahshon, Nahshon the father of Salmon, 21Salmon the father of Boaz, Boaz the father of Obed, 22Obed the father of Jesse, and Jesse the father of David.

ASK

1. Ruth, the foreigner from Moab, is now married to Boaz, and has given birth to a son. This is God's doing; a huge shift of events, altering a whole family's course! (Formerly migrant field worker; now the great grandmother of King David.) Reflect on Ruth's character and heart here. What was it in Ruth that welcomed the powerful broad stroke of God's action and approval that not only changed her life circumstance but also her family line's circumstance, and ultimately the world's circumstance?

2. Would you be willing to invite the Holy Spirit right now to help you reflect on your own heart and character, thanking Him that YOU, like Ruth may be God's choice to shake things up in the world around you? Record your thoughts here.

3. In today's verses we also see life turning around for Naomi, formerly known as "Mara" or "bitter." Could you name something specific that God has made BETTER, erasing the BITTER?

4. What stood out to you most in your study of Ruth? Name a few of your biggest takeaways from this amazing book.

YIELD

Jesus, from today's Scripture reading, is there anything you may be asking me to pay attention to in my own life that would require me to yield?

- Jesus, family relationships matter. Obviously Naomi's relationship with Ruth altered history for all mankind. Is there anything You are asking me to notice or be mindful of in my family relationships?

- Jesus, family legacies matter and family genealogies matter. Is there anything you are asking me to do to invest more thoughtfully in my family legacy?

- Jesus, is there anything you desire to say to me or remind me of regarding my "PRAYER" practices for my family or "PRAYER" practice for YOUR global family?

Help me Jesus to YIELD and to TRUST you.

THE EDGE

King David, the last person mentioned in the Book of Ruth and great-grandson of Ruth and Boaz, wrote most of the Psalms, was one of Israel's most renown kings, was known as "a man after God's own heart," and preceded God's own Son, Jesus Christ, in His earthly genealogy forming the line of David.

Prayer: Family of God

Father,
May the height and depth
of Your loving-kindness flow
in and out of me
through worship and praise!
Pure worship—in Spirit and Truth!
I bow my head
with thanksgiving;
Your covenant of love keeps me.
You hold me close.
Holy Spirit,
soften my heart to love deeply:
a loyal love,
a steadfast love,
a faithful love,
the covenantal love of Jesus,
the enduring love we saw in Ruth.
Thank you that I am an image bearer
of Your beauty and Your character—
virtues we noticed in Ruth and Boaz.
Forgive me Lord,
for the times I refuse to trust You,
when waves of discouragement
wash over me,
when stressful situations consume me,
when heartache deepens
my disappointment,
You, Jesus, are aware.
You shift my perspective!
You lift me above my circumstances.

You fill me with endurance
because You care.
Thank You
for revealing to me
my own heart,
for refining my faith,
for demonstrating Your faithfulness
through difficulty and trials.
You are my Redeemer!
You are HOPE in despair.
You bring fullness to things
that are empty.
You welcome me into your family—
God's Family—
where I find provision, protection,
and all things needed.
MY Kinsman-Redeemer,
Ruth's Kinsman-Redeemer,
the ONE we hoped for
and noticed so long ago
in an "unsandaling" ceremony
by Bethlehem's city gate.
May I give away
the good things You give me,
May I live humbly,
not fearing vulnerability.
May I always be trustworthy,
kind, and loving,
just like Ruth and Boaz.
Equip me with everything good

for doing Your will.
Work in me that which is pleasing to You
so that I, too, may participate
in Your redemptive plan.
Through Jesus Christ,
my Redeemer, Savior, and Lord,
to whom be glory and honor
forever and ever.
Amen.

Prayers & Reflections

Made in United States
Orlando, FL
15 October 2023

37906351R00040